I0806360

Primary Sources of the Civil Rights Movement

Booker T. Washington and the Tuskegee Institute

Budd Bailey

Cavendish Square
New York

Published in 2017 by Cavendish Square Publishing, LLC
243 5th Avenue, Suite 136, New York, NY 10016

Copyright © 2017 by Cavendish Square Publishing, LLC

First Edition

No part of this publication may be reproduced, stored in a retrieval system, or transmitted in any form or by any means—electronic, mechanical, photocopying, recording, or otherwise—without the prior permission of the copyright owner. Request for permission should be addressed to Permissions, Cavendish Square Publishing, 243 5th Avenue, Suite 136, New York, NY 10016. Tel (877) 980-4450; fax (877) 980-4454.

Website: cavendishsq.com

This publication represents the opinions and views of the author based on his or her personal experience, knowledge, and research. The information in this book serves as a general guide only. The author and publisher have used their best efforts in preparing this book and disclaim liability rising directly or indirectly from the use and application of this book.

CPSIA Compliance Information: Batch #CS16CSQ

All websites were available and accurate when this book was sent to press.

Cataloging-in-Publication Data

Names: Bailey, Budd.
Title: Booker T. Washington and the Tuskegee Institute / Budd Bailey.
Description: New York : Cavendish Square, 2017. | Series: Primary sources of the civil rights movement | Includes index.
Identifiers: ISBN 9781502618726 (library bound) | ISBN 9781502618733 (ebook)
Subjects: LCSH: Washington, Booker T.,--1856-1915--Juvenile literature. | Tuskegee Institute--Juvenile literature.
Classification: LCC E185.97.W4 B35 2017 | DDC 370'.92--dc23

Editorial Director: David McNamara
Editor: Fletcher Doyle
Copy Editor: Nathan Heidelberger
Art Director: Jeffrey Talbot
Designer: Amy Greenan
Production Assisant: Karol Szymczuk
Photo Research: J8 Media

The photographs in this book are used by permission and through the courtesy of: Harris & Ewing/Library of Congress/File:Booker T Washington retouched flattened-crop.jpg/Wikimedia Commons, cover; Everett Historical/Shutterstock.com, 5, 13, 35; Frances Benjamin Johnson/Library of Congress, 6, 10, 16; National Park Service, 8; Hulton Archive/Getty Images, 9, 45; Library of Congress, 14, 20 top, 23, 27, 33, 41, 48; Arthur P. Bedou/Robert Abbott Sengstacke/Archive Photos/Getty Images, 18; B.W. Kilburn Company/Library of Congress, 20 bottom; O. Pierre Havens/Lightfoot/Archive Photos/Getty Images, 25; Picture History/Newscom, 29; The Tuskegee University Archives, Tuskegee University, 31; MPI/Archive Photos/Getty Images, 37; John Vachon/PhotoQuest/Archive Photos/Getty Images, 39; Harris & Ewing/Library of Congress, 43; Don Cravens/The LIFE Images Collection/Getty Images, 47; Carol M. Highsmith/Library of Congress, 51.

Printed in the United States of America

CONTENTS

INTRODUCTION

Down Freedom's Road

Anyone who has received an education in the United States in the last 150 years or so can recite a simple lesson: Abraham Lincoln freed the slaves.

That is true. A presidential order called the Emancipation Proclamation went into effect on January 1, 1863. It stated that any slave under the control of the **Confederate States of America**, who had left the United States and was fighting the Civil War with the Union, would be considered "free" in the eyes of the US government. But how could Lincoln free the slaves who lived in the Confederacy?

The Emancipation Proclamation offered a framework for the status of slaves once they lived in the United States again. It prompted some slaves to try to flee for the North, and those who succeeded were instantly considered free when they crossed into US territory. The action solved one of the major problems of the Civil War. It also put the United States government firmly on the side of ending slavery, making the

Abraham Lincoln (*third from left*) reads the Emancipation Proclamation to top government officials in 1862.

conflict much more than a disagreement between neighbors. The Confederacy lost the war in 1865, and an estimated three million slaves were freed.

Now, picture yourself as a former slave. In theory, you were free to do anything you wanted, but in reality, your options were limited. You probably had little or no education. You had a few skills, perhaps because you had done manual labor on a farm. You had no money. If you stayed in the South, you'd run into the same people who always had thought you were less than human simply because of the color of your skin. Freedom was only a first step on the road to equality, and you wondered if you'd ever live to see that equality.

How should African Americans travel down that road? That's one of the most important and lingering questions

Booker T. Washington rose from a childhood of slavery to become one of the most influential African Americans and most recognizable civil rights leaders in the world.

in the history of the United States. Several people have had ideas on that subject. Booker T. Washington was one of the most interesting people to be part of the discussion.

Washington believed that education was the key for blacks to rise in society. There were arguments along the way, and progress was painfully slow. Eventually, though, gains were made in a fight that continues to this day. We celebrate Washington and his contributions for his role in that fight. If you draw a line from Abraham Lincoln to Barack Obama, it touches on the life of Washington.

Let's take a look, then, at Washington's story—his rise from a poor former slave to one of the leading spokesmen of his race in the country, and the decline of his influence in the later years of his life. We'll explore primary sources of information, from Washington's books and speeches to the views of those at the time who agreed and disagreed with his approach for improving the lives of African Americans.

Along the way, we'll find that Washington's words are still relevant, even more than one hundred years after his death in 1915.

CHAPTER ONE

Early Days

Let's take a little road trip.

We leave from Roanoke, Virginia, located in the foothills of the Appalachian Mountains. We drive about 25 miles (40 kilometers) to the southeast, eventually arriving in Hardy, Virginia, which is part of Franklin County.

There sits the Booker T. Washington National Monument. The area is set up to show what life was like in the first few years after Washington's birth in April 1856.

Washington wrote in his book *Up from Slavery*—the autobiography that serves as the best source of information about the first half of his life—that he was born "in a typical log cabin, about fourteen by sixteen feet [4.25 by 5 meters] square. In this cabin I lived with my mother and a brother and sister till after the Civil War." His mother was named Jane. The identity of Booker's father is unknown, and Booker didn't have a last name in the first part of his life.

Washington spent the first few years of his life at a farm in Hardy, Virginia. The area eventually was designated as the Booker T. Washington National Monument.

After Abraham Lincoln's election as president in 1860, eleven Southern states, including Virginia, left the Union. The Civil War began in 1861. When the North defeated the South in 1865, everything changed for Booker and his family. It's stirring to read his first-person description of his reaction to hearing what the Emancipation Proclamation meant for him.

> After the reading we were told that we were all free, and could go when and where we pleased. My mother, who was standing by my side, leaned over and kissed her children, while tears of joy ran down her cheeks … For some minutes there was great rejoicing, and thanksgiving, and wild scenes of ecstasy.

However, the meaning of freedom soon sunk in for ex-slaves. Washington wrote, "The great responsibility of being free, of having charge of themselves, of having to think and plan for themselves and their children, seemed to take possession of them … These were the questions of a home, a living, the rearing of children, education, citizenship, and the establishment and support of churches."

The lives of blacks in the South remained very difficult even after slavery. These African-American moss pickers worked in Savannah, Georgia.

Jane chose to join her husband, Washington Ferguson, who had moved to Malden, West Virginia, during the war. That state had separated from Virginia during the Civil War and joined the Union. Jane brought her children along.

It was illegal in the old South for slaves to go to school; Booker's mother once told him that it would be "dangerous" for a black even to know how to read and write. But Booker had a thirst for education, and he entered school for the first time around the age of ten. Booker also earned money as a teen by working in coal mines and salt furnaces. Later, Booker became a houseboy in the home of a family that owned one of the furnaces.

Along the way, Booker realized he needed a last name, and decided to use the first name of his stepfather as a last name in tribute to him. Jane told Booker that she had called him "Booker Taliaferro" when he was born, and Booker took Taliaferro as a middle name.

Hampton Institute was one of the first colleges in the South to welcome African Americans and Native Americans.

A Tough Trip

In 1872, Washington heard about a college for blacks called Hampton Normal and Agricultural Institute in Hampton, Virginia, near Norfolk. He had a little money saved up and received permission from his mother to go. Washington later wrote when he started he didn't even know exactly where the school was. He begged for rides, slept on the ground, and walked when necessary. Washington looked terrible at the end of the 500-mile (805 km) trip. He had fifty cents in his pocket when he finally reached the university. The assistant principal,

Mary Mackie, asked him to sweep one of the schoolrooms. Washington swept and dusted the area several times, making it spotless. Mackie immediately approved him for admission to Hampton.

Washington completed his studies there in 1875. He knew how important an education had been for him, and he wanted to pass those lessons along to others. However, it took him a while to find the right place to do that. Washington returned home to Malden after graduation to teach school. He also attended Wayland Seminary in Washington, DC, for about eight months in 1878, but he thought the school did not put enough emphasis on industrial training. A year later, Washington was invited to speak at Hampton's graduation ceremony, and shortly after that, Hampton principal General Samuel Armstrong offered him a job on the faculty. Washington accepted the offer. He was happy in that position and probably could have stayed at Hampton for the rest of his life, but events taking place in another part of the country would lead him to a greater challenge.

The United States had spent twelve years rebuilding the former states of the Confederacy; the process has been called **Reconstruction**. The economy of the region had completely collapsed as the end of the Civil War approached in 1865. Reconstruction was a memorable period for African Americans, partly because of a series of new laws. They were allowed to vote for the first time. Three constitutional amendments were passed to ensure more rights for blacks. Hiram Revels was selected in 1870 by the South Carolina state legislature as the first black member of the United States Senate. In that same year, Joseph Rainey was elected to the House of Representatives in South Carolina, the first black to be directly elected to Congress.

But improvements in the lives of African Americans did not last long. Federal troops had been sent to occupy the South, restore law and order, and aid in the rebuilding process.

After several years, many in the North became tired of having troops remain far from home. The economy crashed in 1873, and the expense of rebuilding the South came under attack. It made the end of Reconstruction almost inevitable.

Unfortunate Compromise

The presidential election of 1876 was a close one, and charges of cheating were thrown at both the Republicans and Democrats. A committee was created to sort out the results. Republican Rutherford B. Hayes was declared the winner over Democrat Samuel Tilden, but even that didn't solve all of the problems. Eventually, the two sides worked out a compromise. Hayes took office as president. Troops were pulled out of the South, and disputed elections involving governor's races in some of the former Confederate states were awarded to Democrats.

By 1877, whites had regained political control of the states of the South, and they used every weapon at their disposal to put blacks "in their place." African Americans weren't slaves anymore, but many Southern whites still thought blacks were an inferior race. In the coming years, whites would use violence and intimidation whenever possible to maintain their dominance.

That brings us to 1880 in Alabama. W. F. Foster, a white Democratic state senator, asked Lewis Adams, a local black craftsman, how to gain the support of African Americans in Macon County. Adams requested that a school be built for blacks. A deal was struck, and the Alabama legislature created a college that would be called the **Tuskegee Normal and Industrial Institute.** The state gave the school $2,000 for funding for teachers.

The next step was to find someone to lead the college. State officials contacted Armstrong at the Hampton Institute. Armstrong, a white man, had commanded the Eighth

Frederick Douglass

Frederick Douglass preceded Booker T. Washington in the fight for civil rights for people of color in the United States.

Booker T. Washington was hardly the first African American to work to improve the lives of the members of his race. Frederick Douglass preceded Washington and inspired many blacks to improve their lives.

Born in 1818, Douglass was a slave in Talbot County, Maryland, across the Chesapeake Bay from Washington, DC. He moved to Baltimore as a teen, learned to read and write, and headed north to escape slave status at the age of twenty.

In 1845, Douglass wrote his autobiography, *Narrative of the Life of Frederick Douglass*, which became a bestseller. He also worked on several **abolitionist** newspapers, including the *North Star*. Douglass became the most famous person of color in America. He conferred with President Abraham Lincoln on civil rights issues and later was a representative of the United States in the country's relations with the Dominican Republic and Haiti.

Douglass also worked on issues such as women's rights and Irish home rule over the years. He died in Washington in 1895 and is buried in Rochester, New York.

US Colored Troops in the Civil War. He had developed an interest in the status of blacks, which eventually led him to Hampton. Washington wrote of Armstrong in his autobiography, "One might have removed from Hampton all the buildings, class-rooms, teachers, and industries, and given the men and women there the opportunity of coming into daily contact with General Armstrong, and that alone would have been a liberal education."

General Samuel Armstrong helped Booker T. Washington in a number of ways over the years.

Armstrong advised the Tuskegee Institute to appoint Washington. A telegram came back quickly: "Booker T. Washington will suit us. Send him at once." Washington had enjoyed teaching others, but now he would have the chance to lead an entire college.

Tuskegee was a small town located about 35 miles (56 km) east of Montgomery. Washington's first task was the biggest: the construction of the college itself. Tuskegee Normal and Industrial Institute opened for business on July 4, 1881. The classrooms and offices were temporarily located in a small building located next to a church. The institute had one teacher and thirty students on the first day of school.

A Helping Hand

Within a year, Washington had found a spot for a campus on a former plantation. The cost was $500, steep for a college that had no money. Washington wrote in his book that he received a $250 personal loan from his friend, General J. F. B. Marshall, the treasurer of the Hampton Institute. "I confess that the securing of this money in this way was a great surprise to me, as well as a source of gratification," Washington wrote.

The land was eventually purchased and the institute moved there. The students not only started to receive an education there, but they also learned some crafts, such as making the very bricks used to construct the buildings. They also raised crops and livestock, partly for their own needs and partly for the educational experience.

Washington's idea was to prepare Tuskegee graduates as teachers who would return to their communities and pass on the skills they had learned. However, most of the schools for blacks in those towns were in terrible condition. State governments in the South often had little interest in educating blacks. Washington had the architectural students at Tuskegee come up with blueprints for new schools in the region. He also raised money for their construction.

Washington thought that given an education, blacks could become responsible members of society. From there, they would gain acceptance by whites and slowly move up the economic ladder from severe poverty. There would be no quick gains from that approach. Blacks were not going to be equal to whites at that point in history, and they wouldn't be equal in the relatively near future, but with patience and focus, they could eventually mix in with the rest of the population.

There were success stories. Washington wrote this paragraph in an 1896 *Atlantic* magazine article:

> I wish my readers could have the chance that I have had of going into this community. I wish they could look into the faces of the people and see them beaming with hope and delight. I wish they could see the two or three room cottages that have taken the place of the usual one-room cabin, the well-cultivated farms, and

Students at Tuskegee Institute learned skills by constructing their own college buildings.

> the religious life of the people that now means something more than the name.

It was a reasonable, sound, and logical approach toward trying to solve a difficult situation. No wonder it was applauded in many places. The Tuskegee Institute slowly grew, and its fame grew right along with it. By 1892, the Alabama legislature gave the institute permission to act independently of the state.

Even so, patience is not handed out in equal doses to all. Those who sought immediate equality were in no mood to wait years and years. It led to a conflict that lasted for decades.

CHAPTER TWO

The Speech

American history teaches us many lessons, but there's one that sometimes surprises us no matter how many times we are reminded of it: never underestimate the power of a great speech.

Many leaders have come to prominence with their ability to talk to the public. It could be argued that Barack Obama might never have been president of the United States had he not been so good at making speeches. He used a combination of written words that were powerful and a delivery that echoed a Southern black preacher's patterns. Before Obama, Ronald Reagan was an actor before entering politics, and he was nicknamed "The Great Communicator" once he reached the White House. He was asked if his acting skills helped him as president, and he answered that he didn't know how anyone got by in that job without them.

Booker T. Washington's speeches always were thoughtful and well delivered. He is shown addressing a large crowd in Louisiana.

It was true in Booker T. Washington's day, too. One of the most famous speeches in American history was given by William Jennings Bryan in 1896 during the Democratic National Convention. It turned him into a national figure literally overnight. Bryan was nominated by the Democrats for president the next day. The thirty-six-year-old lost that election, but he repeated what became known as the **"Cross of Gold"** speech to audiences across the country for the next quarter-century.

Washington's speech in Atlanta in 1895 proved memorable and significant. A relatively short address at an exposition changed his life for good, sometimes in unexpected ways. He devotes a full chapter in his autobiography, *Up from Slavery*, to it.

Washington already had established a reputation around the country as a gifted speaker. He accepted many speaking engagements in his life as he raised funds for his school. Simply keeping the institute financially healthy was a big job for one man—the school was sometimes close to financial ruin. So Washington may not have had the time to think about more than speaking and money matters during his first decade at Tuskegee.

A couple of years before the famous Atlanta speech, Washington wrote that he had been looking for the chance to speak directly to a white audience. He received that opportunity in 1893 when he was invited to talk in the Georgia capital to a group known as the **Christian Workers**.

Washington was scheduled to be in Boston at the time of the speech, and he was asked to talk for only five minutes, but Washington decided it was worth the effort. He took a train to Atlanta, gave the address on race relations, and went right back to Boston. "What I said seemed to be received with favor and enthusiasm," Washington wrote. "A good deal was said about it in different parts of the country. I felt that I had in some degree accomplished my object—that of getting a hearing from the dominant class of the South."

His return to Atlanta in 1895 was made to deliver another speech, this one at the **Cotton States and International Exposition**. It was an ugly name for an event that was a smaller version of a **world's fair**. The South was having economic problems, and it was believed that such an exposition would generate interest in the region, particularly when it came to trade with Central and South American nations. Companies could show their goods to the public this way. The expo also had a midway filled with rides, typical of events of that era that tried to attract entire families. During the event, the University of Georgia played Auburn University

The Manufacturer's Building to the Cotton States Expo welcomed visitors with its magnificent architecture.

in football and Buffalo Bill Cody brought in his famous Wild West Show.

African Americans were barely represented at the World's Fair of 1893 in Chicago, and it created some **backlash**. The Cotton States Expo needed to do better. Washington had made a brief speech earlier in 1895 to urge the fair's organizers to build an exhibit designed to showcase the work of African Americans, and the federal government agreed to help pay for such a structure. While eleven buildings were constructed for the exposition, one in particular—the Atlanta Negro building—received a great deal of attention. It was designed to display the achievements and abilities of blacks in the South.

The Atlanta Negro Building at the expo was a chance for blacks to show others some of their accomplishments during the previous thirty years.

Tough Audience

As a leader of the South's black community, Washington was a natural choice to speak at the opening day of the exposition. He was nervous before leaving Tuskegee a day before the speech. "I felt a good deal as I suppose a man feels when he is on his way to the gallows," he wrote. Washington wrote that a white man spoke to him about the problems of speaking before both races at once. "I am afraid that you've got yourself in a tight place," the man said. Washington didn't disagree.

Washington stayed at a **boarding house** in Atlanta. When he awoke on the morning of his speech, he knew the stakes were high. First impressions are always important. Washington knew that there would be many important people from the South in the audience that day. What's more, he realized that he could have served as a slave to some of those people had it not been for the course of history in the previous thirty-five years.

Washington took part in a parade to the exposition grounds, joining black soldiers and prominent citizens in carriages. It was so hot that Washington wrote that he felt "as if I were ready to collapse, and … that my address was not going to be a success." His mere presence shocked some people who hadn't heard that there would be a black speaker. Washington noticed that the room was completely filled. He sat through several speeches, and he probably perspired as he waited for his turn to speak. Finally, former Georgia governor Rufus Bullock introduced him to the crowd: "We now shall be favored by an address by a great Southern educator."

Washington stepped up to the lectern, greeted by an ovation from the blacks and a sprinkle of polite applause from the whites. When he looked out on the large audience, he saw a white and black crowd ready to listen. The two groups didn't sit together—that was years away—but they did hear the same speech.

Washington began with words of thanks to the exposition's organizers, who had allowed blacks to be part of the fair:

> I but convey to you, Mr. President and Directors, the sentiment of the masses of my race when I say that in no way have the value and manhood of the American Negro been more fittingly and generously recognized than by the managers of this magnificent Exposition at every stage of its progress. It is a recognition that will do more to cement the friendship of the two races than any occurrence since the dawn of our freedom.

His calm approach helped dispel any anger among members of the audience.

Washington spoke about how, after the Civil War, blacks first took places in Congress and weren't ready for them. Soon the office holders lost their jobs, and many African Americans had lost their right to vote. "Ignorant and inexperienced, it is not strange that in the first years of our new life we began at the top instead of at the bottom," he said. It was something of an admission from Washington that blacks needed more experience before they were ready to assume the full duties of citizenship. It was a remark guaranteed to receive approval from white audience members.

Then he told a story about a ship that signaled to another ship that it was out of water. The response was "Cast down your bucket where you are." When the first ship did that, it came up with clean water from the Amazon River. Then Washington explained the analogy:

> To those of my race who depend on bettering their condition in a foreign land or who underestimate the importance of cultivating friendly relations with the Southern white

Run Out of Georgia

Rufus Bullock is one of the most interesting yet little known political figures of the nineteenth century.

Born near Albany, New York, he took a job in Augusta, Georgia, in 1860. The Civil War started the next year, and Bullock served as a lieutenant colonel for the Confederacy. After the war, he entered politics. Bullock was a surprise Republican winner in the 1868 election for governor of Georgia, defeating Confederate general and Democrat John Gordon. Bullock was carried to victory by the black vote, but his support for African-American voting rights didn't go over well with many whites. He resigned under mounting pressure in 1870 and left the state.

Bullock later returned to Georgia, was cleared of corruption charges, and became president of Atlanta's first **cotton mill**. He led an effort to stage a large exposition in Georgia in 1895 and asked Booker T. Washington to speak there.

Rufus Bullock was a politician and businessman who was a leader in the fight for civil rights in Georgia.

Bullock died in 1907. He was the last governor in Georgia to fully support equal rights for blacks until future president Jimmy Carter was elected in 1970.

> man, who is their next-door neighbor, I would say: 'Cast down your bucket where you are'—cast it down in making friends in every manly way of the people of all races by whom we are surrounded.

That was a very important issue at the time. Keep in mind that African Americans had enjoyed the benefits of liberty after the Civil War, and then lost them to Jim Crow laws. Life in the South was a little better than in the days of slavery, but not much better. Many African Americans decided to head north instead of staying. The **migration** had grown by the time of Washington's speech. African Americans were headed in large numbers to cities such as New York, Detroit, and Chicago. There they were joined by large numbers of immigrants from southern and eastern European countries. They all went to the back of the economic line upon arrival, and they still faced some forms of discrimination, but many discovered that the opportunity for advancement was greater in the North than in the South.

Still, many didn't make that long trip, perhaps because they couldn't even afford it. The price of cotton in 1895 was close to a fifteen-year low, at $7.62 a pound, making it that much more difficult for black cotton farmers who were leasing land from white owners to make any money. Washington stressed in his speech how important it was that these people be lifted out of the poverty:

> Nearly sixteen millions of hands will aid you in pulling the load upward, or they will pull against you [and push] the load downward. We shall constitute one-third and more of the ignorance and crime of the South, or one-third [of] its intelligence and progress; we shall contribute one-third to the business and industrial prosperity of the South, or we shall

The Southern economy of 1895 relied on the cotton industry. African Americans did much of the work and received very little of the income.

> prove a veritable body of death, stagnating, depressing, retarding every effort to advance the body politic.

It was a way of pointing out to white members of the audience that they had a stake in the economic status of blacks, too. Ignoring them, or stopping their economic progress, would hurt everyone. Washington then used an analogy that has been used in other ways since then:

> In all things that are purely social, we can be as separate as the fingers, yet one as the hand in all things essential to mutual progress.

Dignity in Work

In the meantime, he was willing to admit that blacks probably had to work their way up the economic ladder, starting from their present spot on the bottom. "No race can prosper till it learns that there is as much dignity in tilling a field as in writing a poem," he said.

Near the end, Washington said, "It is important and right that all privileges of the law be ours, but it is vastly more important that we be prepared for the exercises of those privileges. The opportunity to earn a dollar in a factory just now is worth infinitely more than the opportunity to spend a dollar in an opera-house." It was considered by some an offer of a compromise—blacks would accept segregation and the loss of political rights in exchange for economic opportunity.

The cheering was long and loud. Kelefa Sanneh of the *New Yorker* magazine wrote in 2009 that Washington had allowed both whites and blacks to cheer for themselves with this well-crafted speech. The whites could voice approval for the idea that blacks needed to make economic progress, thus looking open minded. They could applaud the idea that an educated African American had concluded that segregation of the races in the South did not have to end immediately. Blacks could applaud the idea that they needed to move up the economic ladder in order to make everyone's lives better. There weren't many people in the South in 1895 who could pull off the trick of making whites and blacks applaud the same speech, in the same arena, at the same time. Washington had done that.

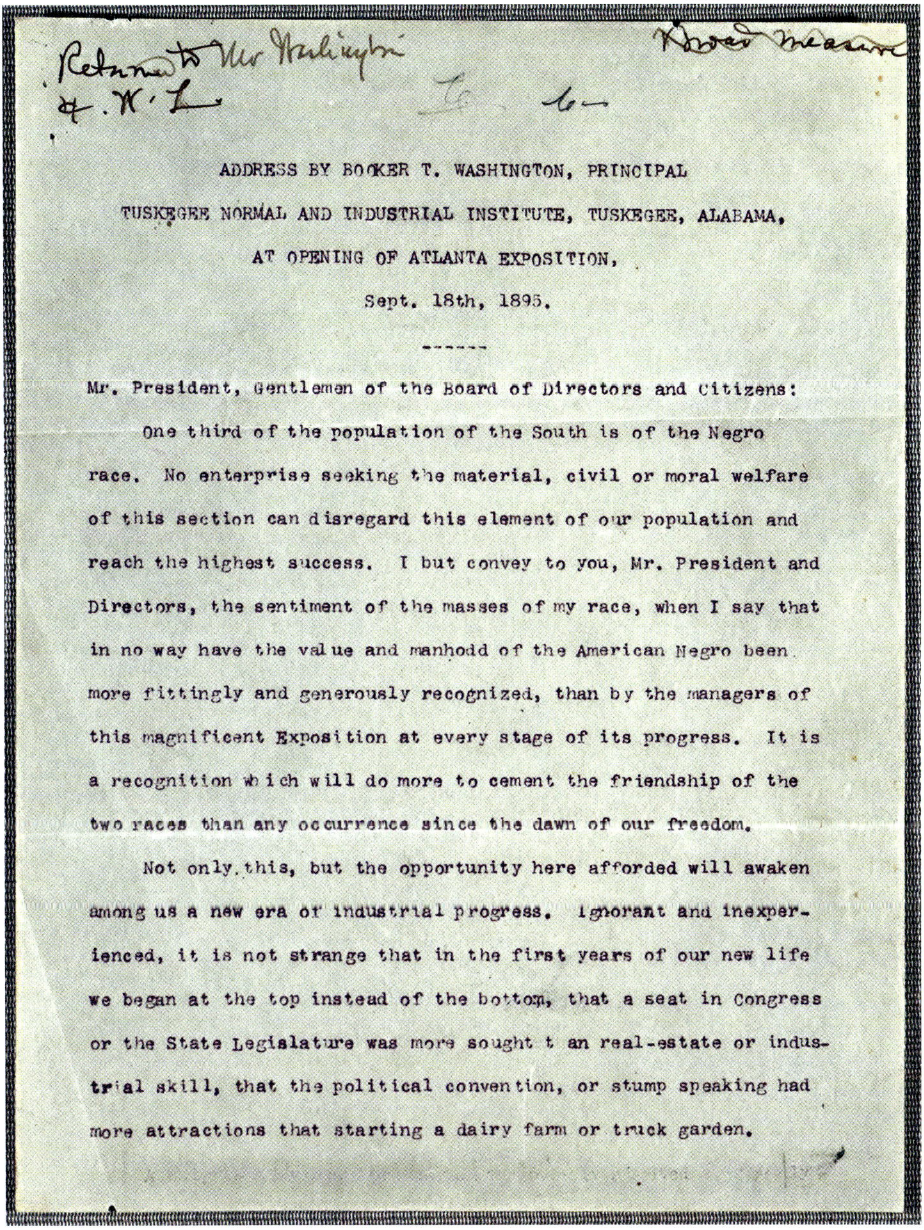

ADDRESS BY BOOKER T. WASHINGTON, PRINCIPAL

TUSKEGEE NORMAL AND INDUSTRIAL INSTITUTE, TUSKEGEE, ALABAMA,

AT OPENING OF ATLANTA EXPOSITION,

Sept. 18th, 1895.

Mr. President, Gentlemen of the Board of Directors and Citizens:

One third of the population of the South is of the Negro race. No enterprise seeking the material, civil or moral welfare of this section can disregard this element of our population and reach the highest success. I but convey to you, Mr. President and Directors, the sentiment of the masses of my race, when I say that in no way have the value and manhodd of the American Negro been more fittingly and generously recognized, than by the managers of this magnificent Exposition at every stage of its progress. It is a recognition which will do more to cement the friendship of the two races than any occurrence since the dawn of our freedom.

Not only this, but the opportunity here afforded will awaken among us a new era of industrial progress. Ignorant and inexperienced, it is not strange that in the first years of our new life we began at the top instead of the bottom, that a seat in Congress or the State Legislature was more sought t an real-estate or industrial skill, that the political convention, or stump speaking had more attractions that starting a dairy farm or truck garden.

This is an image of the original copy of Booker T. Washington's famous speech in 1895 in Atlanta.

The result was electric. In Washington's autobiography, he writes about how Bullock immediately came over to shake his hand—and many others joined in that show of support. Washington had trouble getting past the numerous well-wishers to leave the building. The enthusiasm of people continued a day later in Atlanta's business district. "I was surprised to find myself pointed out and surrounded by a crowd of men who wished to shake hands with me," he wrote. When Washington headed back to Tuskegee by train, he found crowds waiting for him at every stop.

Speech Reprinted

The speech was reprinted in its entirety in the *Springfield Republican* in Massachusetts, and celebrated in editorials by many newspapers. Washington quotes the *Boston Transcript* in his book: "The speech of Booker T. Washington at the Atlanta Exposition, this week, seems to have dwarfed all the other proceedings and the Exposition itself. The sensation that it has caused in the press has never been equaled." A few days later, Washington sent a copy of his speech to the sitting president of the United States, Grover Cleveland. The president's thank-you note was written on October 6: "Your words cannot fail to delight and encourage all who wish well for your race."

Washington also received a note of congratulations from a man named William Edward Burghardt (W. E. B.) Du Bois. He described the speech as "a word fitly spoken." Du Bois would have much more to say about the speech in the years to come, much of it critical in nature. A loud and long debate about Washington's plan to improve the lives of African Americans was about to begin. Washington, meanwhile, gave variations of that speech to audiences for the final twenty years of his life.

Alabama governor William Oates offered African Americans with a college degree little hope for advancement.

And while some whites were enthusiastic about Washington's approach, others were not. In 1897, Governor William Oates of Alabama addressed the Tuskegee graduation ceremony:

> You might as well understand that this is a white man's country, as far as the South is concerned, and we are going to make you keep your place. Understand that. I have nothing more to say to you.

Washington's self-defined task would be a difficult one.

CHAPTER THREE

Opposite Reactions

No one would have thought to use the word at this point in history, but Booker T. Washington had become a superstar.

In 1896, Washington accepted an honorary master's degree from Harvard University, the first African American to do so. When he received the invitation, Washington wrote that:

> As I sat upon my veranda, with this letter in my hand, tears came to my eyes. My whole former life—my life as a slave on the plantation, my work in the coal-mine, the times when I was without food and clothing, when I made my bed under a sidewalk, my struggles for an education … the ostracism and sometimes oppression of my race—all this passed before me and nearly overcame me.

He was invited to speak all across the country after the Atlanta speech. In 1897, he was asked to appear at the

Booker T. Washington sat for a photograph during his visit to Boston, where he became the first African American to receive an honorary master's degree from Harvard University.

dedication of the Robert Gould Shaw Memorial in Boston. Shaw was the leader of the Fifty-Fourth Regiment for the Union Army during the Civil War, and that group was one of the first African-American units to see action. Shaw was killed in the fighting. Washington's appearance was the highlight of the ceremony. "When this man of culture and voice and power, as well as a dark skin, began … feeling began to mount," the *Boston Transcript* reported. "You could see tears glisten in the eyes of soldiers and civilians."

When Washington started Tuskegee, he made a vow to himself that he would make the institute such an impressive facility that even the president of the United States would visit. In 1898, Washington heard that President William McKinley was considering a trip to Atlanta. A ceremony was planned to mark the successful conclusion of the Spanish-American War. Washington took a trip to the nation's capital and went to the White House. The president agreed to meet with him briefly. McKinley said he wasn't sure about the details of his Atlanta trip, but asked to have the matter of a visit to Tuskegee called to his attention in a few weeks.

Washington did that by going back to the nation's capital for another meeting with McKinley, and the president agreed to visit Tuskegee on December 16, 1898. The town never had a bigger day. Tuskegee was thoroughly decorated, and a parade was held in the president's honor. Later, McKinley spoke of how the Tuskegee Normal and Industrial Institute had received acclaim across the country and throughout parts of the world. Then the president spoke about his host:

> To speak of Tuskegee without paying special tribute to Booker T. Washington's genius and perseverance would be impossible. The inception of this noble enterprise was his, and he deserves high credit for it … He has won a worthy reputation as one of the great leaders of his race, widely known and much respected at home and abroad as an accomplished educator, a great orator, and a true philanthropist.

What could top that? Perhaps a personal invitation to dine at the White House would qualify as an equal or greater honor for Washington. One would be made, but not from McKinley.

Theodore Roosevelt's career had one of the fastest ascents in American political history. In 1895, he served as the head

President William McKinley enjoys a huge welcome during an 1898 visit to the Tuskegee Institute. He is standing on the train platform between Alabama governor Joseph Johnston and Booker T. Washington.

of the Board for New York City Police Commissioners. That led to a job as assistant secretary of the navy in 1897. When war broke out with Spain in April 1898, Roosevelt resigned his position to join the American forces. He became a hero in the four-month war, returned to the United States, and successfully ran for governor of New York that November.

Once in office, Roosevelt was a popular speaker, and he spoke at the same event as Washington at least once. The two men got along well, and exchanged letters on race relations. Roosevelt became McKinley's choice to be vice president when McKinley ran for reelection in 1900, as the previous vice president, Garret Hobart, had died in 1899. McKinley and Roosevelt won, but McKinley was in office only until September 1901. The president visited the **Pan-American Exposition** in Buffalo, New York. McKinley was shaking hands at a public appearance when shot by Leon Czolgosz, an **anarchist**. The president died later that month. Roosevelt was then sworn in as president of the United States.

Invitation to the White House

It took him less than a month to do something no president had ever done: formally invite a man of color to the White House to dine. Roosevelt is said to have told a friend that he wasn't sure whether he should invite a black man to the president's official residence. Then Roosevelt felt such shame over those feelings that he immediately wrote a letter to Washington. "When are you coming north? I must see you as soon as possible. I want to talk over the question of future appointments exactly on the lines of our last conversation together," he wrote.

The date was set for October 16, 1901, with race relations and the government policy in the South on the agenda. The next day, the White House issued a statement that the president and his family had had dinner with Washington.

The reaction was swift and vicious. Some people were particularly shocked that Roosevelt's seventeen-year-old daughter, Alice, ate at the same table with a black man in the White House. One unidentified Chicago newspaper printed this letter from a white reader:

> Every Southern man of intelligence honors Booker T. Washington … but we cannot admit him to social equality, because that involves

This lithograph pays tribute to Booker T. Washington's historic dinner with President Theodore Roosevelt at the White House in 1901.

> a principle which is vital to the preservation of the Southern white race from the evils of intermarriage with blacks.

The comments were even harsher in the South. The *Biloxi Daily Herald* in Mississippi wrote, "The most damnable outrage which has ever been perpetrated by any citizen of the United States was committed by the president when he invited a negro to dine with him at the White House." One letter writer to Mississippi's *Jackson Clarion-Ledger* wrote, "I have more respect for the blackest, rankest-smelling chicken thief in Mississippi than I have for the occupant of the White House."

Different Paths to Freedom

When Booker T. Washington addressed a Harvard alumni group in 1896, he summarized his position on improving the status of blacks:

> During the next half century and more, my race must continue passing through the severe American crucible. We are to be tested in our patience, our forbearance, our perseverance, our power to endure wrong, to withstand temptations, to economize, to acquire and use skill; our ability to compete, to succeed in commerce, to disregard the superficial for the real, the appearance for the substance, to be great and yet small, learned and yet simple, high and yet the servant of all … The Negro must possess it, or be debarred.
>
> While we are thus being tested, I beg of you to remember that wherever our life touches yours, we help or hinder. Wherever your life touches ours, you make us stronger or weaker. No member of your race in any part of our country can harm the meanest member of mine, without the proudest and bluest blood in Massachusetts being degraded.

In *The Autobiography of W. E .B. Du Bois*, Du Bois writes of his disagreement with Washington's approach:

> The black men of America have a duty to perform, a duty stern and delicate—a forward movement to oppose a part of the work of their greatest leader. So far as Mr. Washington preaches Thrift, Patience,

W. E. B. Du Bois offered a different path to racial equality and justice than Washington's.

and Industrial Training for the masses, we must hold up his hands and strive with him, rejoicing in his honors and glorying in the strength of this Joshua called of God and of man to lead the headless host.

But so far as Mr. Washington apologizes for injustice, North or South, does not rightly value the privilege and duty of voting, belittles the emasculating effects of caste distinctions, and opposes the higher training and ambition of our brighter minds—so far as he, the South, or the Nation, does this—we must unceasingly and firmly oppose them. By every civilized and peaceful method we must strive for the rights which the world accords to men.

While Washington enjoyed immense personal popularity after his 1895 speech in Atlanta, it's fair to say that his ideas of slow but steady economic progress for race relations weren't as universally accepted. In fact, his speeches were sometimes interrupted by shouts from those who disagreed with his views. While there were blacks who promoted violence against whites as a way to speed up the process, and others who thought a return to Africa by blacks would be an answer, those ideas never gained widespread popularity.

However, a group led by Du Bois thought that a political rather than economic solution was needed. If those forces needed inspiration, it came in the form of an infamous Supreme Court decision less than a year after Washington's speech in Atlanta.

Bad Precedent

Homer Plessy was the subject of a test case concerning segregation laws in the South. He tried to gain a seat in the whites-only section of a train but was told that he had to sit in the so-called colored section. Plessy and his supporting group immediately sued, claiming the action was a violation of his constitutional rights for equal treatment under the law. He lost the first legal round and was fined $25, and he appealed. The landmark case was called *Plessy v. Ferguson*, and it reached the Supreme Court of the United States. The court ruled that separation of the races in public transportation was government policy rather than a violation of the Constitution. It found that "separate but equal" facilities for whites and blacks were legal, which had the effect of segregating the races.

While such facilities as railroad cars, public bathrooms, and schools were certainly separate for blacks and whites, there was nothing equal about them. It is considered one of the worst decisions in Supreme Court history.

Du Bois must have been angered by the decision, and his views soon hardened. Du Bois was a native of Massachusetts,

Railroad stations in the South had separate waiting rooms for blacks and whites as late as the 1960s.

and he graduated from Fisk University and Harvard University, where he received a PhD in history in 1895. He thought that other blacks should follow that example and learn about the liberal arts—English, mathematics, literature, etc.—as a way to better themselves. That was in contrast to Washington's more vocational approach to education. Du Bois also didn't like the relatively cozy arrangement that Washington had developed with other black institutions around the country, and with white politicians in Washington.

Du Bois wrote in *The Souls of Black Folk* in 1903:

> Mr. Washington represents in Negro thought the old attitude of adjustment and submission ... [His] program practically accepts the alleged inferiority of the Negro races.

By 1900, some African Americans were calling Washington's famous speech "The Atlanta Compromise." Washington's offer to not press for certain rights for blacks in exchange for a bit of economic opportunity struck some as the wrong course of action. The *Boston Guardian's* publisher, William Monroe Trotter, spoke of "Washington's crime of race ridicule and belittlement," and compared him to the most famous traitor in American military history, Benedict Arnold. While much of America was familiar with Washington's name, he had begun to lose his status as the leading spokesman for blacks.

Balancing Act

The criticism may not have been fair. Washington's approach could be considered making the best of a terrible situation. After almost two decades of decline in the lives of African Americans, Washington wanted a change of direction. He was trying to practice moderation by pushing blacks forward while not threatening whites. It was a difficult balancing act.

Still, Du Bois believed Washington was not representing blacks properly, and he often attacked his rival in print. One such essay was called "On Mr. Booker T. Washington and Others." Du Bois believed Washington's efforts had led to African Americans becoming distinctly inferior to whites in the eyes of the government, and that Washington had damaged those who wished to better themselves through a more classical education.

By July 1905, Du Bois stepped up his activism. Twenty-nine men assembled north of Buffalo, New York, to create the Niagara Movement, a civil rights group that took the name of the nearby Niagara River. They planned to meet on the American side of Niagara Falls but were denied hotel rooms and moved the gathering to the Canadian side. They hoped that they could create "a strong current of change." Du Bois helped to write a declaration of principles, which included equal status under the law, equal economic opportunities, and an attack on segregation laws in the South. It was an attack on Washington's approach.

Several black leaders who met in 1905 near Niagara Falls to discuss civil rights called themselves "The Founders of the Niagara Movement."

Some black newspapers that were sympathetic to Washington's views tried to downplay the beliefs of the Niagara Movement. Others printed information about the principles of the group, which met again in 1906. The organization had some growth, but it eventually collapsed as disagreements over principles among members took place. By 1909, the Niagara Movement essentially had ceased to exist. However, activists met in New York in that same year to form the National Association for the Advancement of Colored People (NAACP). That group turned out to be a durable one.

Washington and Du Bois never did reach an agreement on how African Americans could advance themselves.

CHAPTER FOUR

Changing Attitudes

The two sides of the debate concerning the best way to obtain civil rights had turned bitter by 1910. Washington didn't like the competition for the role of leader of African Americans. He created something of a network of supporters around the country to promote his viewpoints. It probably started with people who worked at schools similar to Tuskegee, and grew to include other supporters. Washington did have a voice in some **patronage** appointments in government, and wasn't afraid to use it. Still, the Tuskegee leader sometimes made gestures of support to the side backed by W. E. B. Du Bois. He gave money to support certain political and judicial actions.

Through it all, Washington continued his work in education. He received a boost when Julius Rosenwald became very interested in Washington's efforts. Rosenwald was one of the most important businessmen in America at the

Julius Rosenwald of Sears, Roebuck & Co. financially supported the Tuskegee Institute and schools for African-American children.

time, since he served as the president and part owner of **Sears, Roebuck and Co.**

Rosenwald was a rich man who gave much of his money away. He joined the Board of Directors of Tuskegee Institute in 1912 and awarded the school a large amount of money so that Washington could spend less time raising money for the school. In that same year, Rosenwald personally paid for the construction of six small schools in Alabama. It was the start of a much bigger program. "The Rosenwald Fund" was established in 1917. Eventually, that foundation spent more than $29 million building almost five thousand schools for children in fifteen states across the South. By 1932, about one-third of the South's African-American schools were built that way and were called "Rosenwald Schools."

Organizations such as the **National Urban League** were formed to help African Americans in that era, but the times and attitudes of the nation were changing. The 1912 presidential election pitted incumbent Republican William Howard Taft against Democrat Woodrow Wilson and independent candidate Theodore Roosevelt. Taft, who mostly had avoided civil rights issues as president, and Roosevelt split the Republican vote, and a Democrat was elected to the presidency for the first time since 1892.

Southern President

Wilson was a brilliant, complicated man. He continued to bring forth some elements of reform that were associated with Roosevelt, and he fought for liberty overseas. However, his work on race relations was dismal. He was the first native Southerner to be elected president since Zachary Taylor in 1848, and he carried all of the Southern states in the election. Wilson himself is said to have expressed disappointment in the outcome of the Civil War. Wilson soon ordered the segregation of facilities in government buildings. Blacks were frequently passed over for civil service jobs, and others were fired.

Through it all, Washington kept spreading his message. He visited Utah in 1913 to address members of the Church of Jesus Christ of Latter-day Saints. The *University of Utah Chronicle* described the event:

> Greeted by vociferous applause and the largest audience which has attended assembly this year, Booker T. Washington, the renowned Negro writer, orator and educator, appeared before the University Faculty and students Thursday morning. The genuine reception accorded him was so increased by appreciation of his talk that at its conclusion he was called back again to the platform.

However, there were signs that equal rights for blacks weren't a popular cause around the country. In

1915, D. W. Griffith produced a ground-breaking film titled *Birth of a Nation*, which set standards for technical achievements. However, its portrait of American life in the South during Reconstruction is one-sided and wrong. Blacks are shown to be evil and immoral, and the **Ku Klux Klan** rides to the rescue of white Southern citizens at the movie's end. The film damaged race relations across the country and caused a few riots. Yet when Wilson saw the motion picture, he said, "It is like writing history with lightning, and my only regret is that it is all so terribly true."

This still from the pro–Ku Klux Klan movie *Birth of a Nation* shows Klan members suppressing a man portrayed as dangerous to society.

By that point, Washington's time had almost run out. He had been working hard for his cause for decades. By 1915, his health started to deteriorate. Around November 1, Washington collapsed in New York City and was hospitalized. He reportedly asked to return to Tuskegee: "I was born in the South, have lived all my life in the South, and expect to die and be buried in the South." The civil rights leader got his wish as he died in Tuskegee on November 14, 1915, about five hours after arrival. A medical conference in 2006 examined Washington's medical records and judged that he had died of kidney failure that was related to high blood pressure.

Tributes Roll In

The tributes arrived quickly after his death. The *New York Tribune* had a long story on Washington, with a small headline, "Negro educator, ex-Slave, was Moses of His Race."

The *New York Times* printed this statement from Theodore Roosevelt:

> I am deeply shocked and grieved at the death of Dr. Washington. He was one of the distinguished citizens of the United States, a man who rendered greater service to his race than had ever been rendered by any one else, and who, in so doing, also rendered great service to the whole country.

Two of the most famous businessmen of the age, who both had donated money to Washington's work, sent telegrams to Tuskegee praising the educator upon hearing of his death. Oil executive John D. Rockefeller said, "I learn with sorrow of the death of Dr. Washington. Be assured of my sympathy for you in this sudden and sad bereavement. He rendered invaluable services to his race in a life devoted to their uplift and he was most highly appreciated by multitudes of the best people in the land. He will be greatly missed." Steel industrialist Andrew Carnegie said, "I mourn with you today as one who shares your sorrow. America has lost one of her best and greatest citizens. History is to tell of two Washingtons: One the father of his country, the other the leader of his race."

Du Bois also had something to say in the *Crisis*, an NAACP publication. After giving Washington credit as the most distinguished man to come out of the South since the Civil War, he wrote, "In stern justice, we must lay on the soul of

Rosa Parks's simple decision not to move to the back of a bus in 1955 sparked a huge shift in the civil rights movement.

Sparked by Parks

Debates about how to improve the status of African Americans had been taking place for decades by the 1950s. Yet it was a simple gesture by a woman on a bus that provided the spark for what became an explosion of energy and an agent of change.

Rosa Parks was riding a bus after work in Montgomery, Alabama, on December 1, 1955, when she was asked to move to the rear of the bus to make room for a white passenger. Parks refused and was arrested by Montgomery police. She later said that she had grown tired of giving in on such issues.

Martin Luther King Jr. soon organized an effective boycott by blacks of Montgomery's bus system. Some churches were burned, and King's house was bombed in retaliation, but in November 1956, the Supreme Court ruled that the city's policy of having segregated seating on buses was unconstitutional. The boycott ended on December 20, 1956.

The incident became a huge step toward the end of segregation.

Booker T. Washington's coffin is carried to a grave as hundreds in Tuskegee, Alabama, mourn.

this man, a heavy responsibility for the consummation of Negro disfranchisement, the decline of the Negro college and public school, and the firmer establishment of color caste in this land."

Isaac Fisher, a black educator, wrote about the funeral service in Tuskegee for the *Montgomery Advertiser* in Alabama. He reported that Washington "was buried here Wednesday with the same simplicity and lack of studied pomp and ceremony with which God's own hand buried Moses in the land of Moab. No labored eulogies; no boastings of his great work; no gorgeous trappings of horses; no streaming banners; no mysterious ceremonies of lodges."

Fisher's report turned poignant when he described the African Americans who came to the service.

> Most pathetic of all was the sight of the humble and unlettered colored people of the cotton fields who literally packed the school grounds. They had sustained a loss which they did not know how to voice. You could see them looking into every face near them for encouragement to

say how much they were hurt and would miss their devoted friend.

Soon after Washington's death, the NAACP and Washington's supporters realized their differences weren't that large, and cooperation between the two groups increased. But all African Americans had their work cut out for them if they hoped to bring change to society. Wilson was still the president for five more years. When protesters complained about his racial policies toward the army in 1918, Wilson said to them: "Segregation is not a humiliation but a benefit, and ought to be so regarded by you gentlemen."

Black Migration

After the end of World War I in 1918, the nation's mood turned inward and calls for social change were quickly rejected. Thousands of blacks escaped the oppression of the South and moved north. That wave continued for the next twenty years.

During the 1920s, progress toward equality for blacks remained slow. The Ku Klux Klan was at the height of its power, terrorizing and intimidating African Americans in many parts of the country. Segregation was still a fact of life in the South. In the 1930s, many blacks worried more about eating than they worried about voting. The **Great Depression** began in 1929, and African Americans were hit disproportionately hard. Unemployment went above 60 percent for blacks in some areas of the country.

The Depression didn't end in America until the start of World War II in 1941, and millions of men—white and black—went overseas to fight for democracy and against tyranny. After winning the war in 1945, some of those same blacks came back to America and were angered by the fact that they didn't enjoy the benefits of liberty at home. The fight to gain equal rights was about to speed up.

The NAACP played a key role in one of the most famous court cases of the time. Lawyers for the group argued again that separate obviously did not mean equal when it came to schools around the country. This time, justices of the Supreme Court in 1954 unanimously struck down the ruling from *Plessy vs. Ferguson* in a case called *Brown vs. Board of Education of Topeka*. Separate schools for blacks and whites were ruled unconstitutional, and other forms of segregation soon would be outlawed.

Correct Assumption

Washington's methods had fallen out of favor by then as African Americans looked for ways to bring changes more quickly. Many people contributed to the concept of equality in the United States, and major steps were taken in the 1960s toward that goal—about one hundred years after the end of the Civil War. Legislation was passed that guaranteed blacks the right to vote once again, banning such tools as literacy tests that stopped African Americans from voting. Other laws prevented discrimination in housing. Progress came with a great deal of bloodshed. As historian Kelefa Sanneh wrote in the *New Yorker* in 2009, Washington's belief that trying to change the system quickly would lead to violence was proven correct.

Defending Washington's viewpoints hasn't always been popular, but recently there has been more of an understanding that we must look at him as a product of his times. Washington began his life as a slave and rose to become the leader of a university and an advisor to presidents. Few Americans have overcome such handicaps to gain such prominence.

Perhaps the greatest testimony to the legacy of Washington is the success of the Tuskegee Institute. Under Washington, it grew from one building housing one teacher and 30 students to 100 fully equipped buildings housing 200 teachers and 1,500 students learning 40 trades. By the 1920s, the institute switched to a path favored by Du Bois and began focusing on more academic subjects. It became a degree-granting institution. The institute donated land for

Tuskegee University is still educating students—a tribute to Booker T. Washington's vision.

the Tuskegee VA Hospital. When it opened in 1923, it was the first and only facility in the United States staffed by black professionals. A veterinary school was opened that has trained about three-quarters of all African-American veterinarians in the United States. The famed Tuskegee Airmen, four squadrons of African-American fighter pilots who fought with great distinction during World War II, were trained at the institute. The United Negro College Fund was started there. The school became a full university, granting advanced degrees, in 1985.

Washington did his best to try to improve the lives of African Americans. When blacks were near a low point, Washington tried to give them a path toward better days. His feelings were unselfish, heartfelt, and genuine. In the process, he provided blacks with the hope of a better future when they needed it the most. For that, Washington should be remembered by Americans of all races.

Chronology

Dates in green pertain to events discussed in this volume.

1856 Booker T. Washington is born on April 5 in Hale's Ford, Virginia.

1857 The Supreme Court's *Dred Scott* decision rules that blacks have no citizenship rights.

1861 Southern states secede from the Union, leading to the start of the Civil War.

1863 The Emancipation Proclamation is issued by President Abraham Lincoln.

1865 The Thirteenth Amendment, abolishing slavery, is passed in the US House of Representatives. The amendment was passed by the Senate in 1864.

1868 The Fourteenth Amendment, guaranteeing equal rights under the law, is passed.

1870 The Fifteenth Amendment, prohibiting governments from denying male citizens the right to vote based on their race, is passed.

1872 Booker T. Washington walks about 500 miles (804 km) to Hampton, Virginia, and is admitted into Hampton Normal Agricultural Institute.

1877 Reconstruction ends in the South, and many rights for African Americans, such as voting, begin to disappear.

1881 Washington begins work as the head of the Tuskegee Institute in Alabama.

1883 The Supreme Court strikes down the Civil Rights Act of 1875, which guaranteed equal rights to all African Americans in transportation, restaurant or inns, theaters, and on juries.

1895 Booker T. Washington gives a speech at the Cotton States and International Exposition in Atlanta, urging blacks to concentrate on economic rather than political issues.

1896 *Plessy v. Ferguson*, establishing the precedent of "separate but equal," is handed down by the Supreme Court of the United States.

1898 President William McKinley and much of his cabinet pay an official visit to the Tuskegee Institute.

1901 Washington has dinner with President Theodore Roosevelt at the White House.

1905 The Niagara Movement, an attempt to create a different path to racial equality than Washington's, is founded near Buffalo, New York.

1905 President Roosevelt visits Washington in Tuskegee.

1909 The National Association for the Advancement of Colored People (NAACP) is established.

1912 Woodrow Wilson is elected president. He believed segregation of races was good for the nation, and civil rights takes a step backward during his time in office.

1915 Washington dies at the age of fifty-nine in Tuskegee.

1941 President Franklin D. Roosevelt bans discrimination against minorities in the granting of defense contracts.

1947 Jackie Robinson breaks the color barrier, becoming the first African American to play in Major League Baseball.

1954 Thurgood Marshall and the NAACP win the case of *Brown v. Board of Education of Topeka*, which overturns *Plessy v. Ferguson* and the "separate but equal" doctrine of segregation in the United States.

1955 Rosa Parks refuses to give up her seat to a white person on a bus in Montgomery, Alabama. Her arrest sparks a bus boycott that leads to buses being desegregated in that city.

1957 Federal troops are called in to protect nine African-American students in Little Rock, Arkansas, who are trying to attend all-white Central High School.

1961 Congress on Racial Equality organizes Freedom Rides throughout the South, and the riders suffer beatings from mobs in many cities.

1963 The March on Washington attracts a quarter of a million people, who listen to Martin Luther King Jr.'s "I Have a Dream" speech.

1964 President Lyndon B. Johnson signs the Civil Rights Act of 1964. It prohibits discrimination of all kinds.

1965 When an effort to register black voters is met with resistance in the South, Martin Luther King Jr. and the Southern Christian Leadership Conference organize a march for voting rights in Alabama from Selma to Montgomery. Later in the year, Congress passes the Voting Rights Act.

1967 Thurgood Marshall becomes the first African-American Supreme Court justice.

1968 Martin Luther King Jr. is assassinated in Memphis, Tennessee. He is there to support a sanitation workers strike.

1985 Tuskegee achieves full university status and begins granting advanced degrees.

Glossary

abolitionist A person who wanted to abolish or eliminate slavery before the Civil War.

anarchist A person who opposes the idea of government in society. Leaders of France, Austria, Italy, and the United States were killed by anarchists from 1892 to 1901.

backlash A negative reaction to a development in social or political affairs.

boarding house A place that can be rented out by visitors for a day to months at a time. Such places often served meals.

Christian Workers The name of a formal alliance of groups across the United States in the late nineteenth century devoted to performing charitable actions in a variety of locations, including homes, schools, prisons, and churches.

Confederate States of America The formal name of the states that left the United States of America to form a separate country in 1861, starting the Civil War.

cotton mill A machine that turned cotton into cloth and yarn.

Cotton States and International Exposition This smaller version of a world's fair attracted eight hundred thousand people to Atlanta in the fall of 1895. Several states had exhibition halls.

"Cross of Gold" A reference to a speech given by William Jennings Bryan at the 1896 Democratic National Convention. Bryan believed that using silver and gold to support the US dollar would lead to prosperity for the United States.

Great Depression The worst economic situation in the history of the Western industrialized world, lasting roughly from 1929 to 1939. Millions lost their jobs as factories closed.

Ku Klux Klan An organization created after the Civil War to suppress African American rights, often through intimidation. The group later revived around 1915 to add Catholics, Jews, and the foreign-born to its list of targets.

migration A large number of people moving from one place to another.

National Urban League An organization founded in New York City in 1910 that tried to offer assistance to blacks.

Pan-American Exposition A world's fair staged in Buffalo, New York, in 1901.

patronage The power to control appointments to specific government jobs.

Reconstruction The effort by the United States government to rebuild the social, economic, and political systems of the Southern states between 1865 and 1877.

Sears, Roebuck and Co. This company, formed in 1886, got its start through mail order sales.

Tuskegee Normal and Industrial Institute This Alabama college, formed in 1881, was originally called the Normal School for Colored Teachers at Tuskegee. "Normal" indicates that it was a teachers' school.

world's fair A large public exhibition. People from all over the world are invited to take part by displaying their goods and promoting their native lands.

Further Information

Books

Norrell, Robert J. *Up from History: The Life of Booker T. Washington*. Cambridge, MA: The Belknap Press of Harvard University Press, 2009.

Schroeder, Alan. *Booker T. Washington: Educator and Racial Spokesman*. Black Americans of Achievement. New York: Chelsea House, 2004.

Smock, Raymond W. *Booker T. Washington: Black Leadership in the Age of Jim Crow*. Chicago: Ivan R. Dee, 2009.

Washington, Booker T. *My Larger Education: Being Chapters from My Experience*. Mineola, NY: Dover Publications, 2013. First published 1911 by Doubleday, Page and Company.

Washington, Booker T. *Up from Slavery*. Mineola, NY: Dover Publications, 1995. First published 1901 by Doubleday, Page and Company.

Websites

Booker T. Washington Biography—People and Their Lives
www.youtube.com/watch?v=FN0DVsM03Qg

This documentary on Washington offers plenty of photos of the African-American leader and runs more than thirty-five minutes.

Booker T. Washington: Educator, Civil Rights Activist
www.biography.com/people/booker-t-washington-9524663

This is a compact outline of Washington's life from biography.com. It contains links to videos and other websites about Washington.

The Booker T. Washington Society
www.btwsociety.org

This group has been dedicated to promoting Washington's beliefs and agenda since it was created in 2005.

Bibliography

Allen, Nick. "Tea with Teddy: Booker T. Washington and Theodore Roosevelt." History in an Hour. Accessed November 16, 2015. http://www.historyinanhour.com/2010/09/12/booker-t-washington-and-theordore-roosevelt.

American Anthropological Association. "Immigration, Black Migration and U.S. Colonialism." Understanding Race. Accessed November 16, 2015. http://www.understandingrace.org/history/society/immigration.html.

Biography.com editors. "Booker T. Washington Biography." Accessed November 11, 2015. http://www.biography.com/people/booker-t-washington-9524663.

———. "Frederick Douglass Biography." Accessed November 16, 2015. http://www.biography.com/people/frederick-douglass-9278324.

———. "Rosa Parks Biography." Accessed November 16, 2015. http://www.biography.com/people/rosa-parks-9433715.

Booker T. Washington Society. "Honorary Master of Arts Degree." Accessed December 11, 2015. http://www.btwsociety.org/library/honors/01.php.

"B. T. Washington Dead." *New York Tribune*, November 15, 1915. Accessed November 29, 2015. http://chroniclingamerica.loc.gov/lccn/sn83030214/1915-11-15/ed-1/seq-1.

Du Bois, W. E. B. *The Autobiography of W. E. B. Du Bois*. New York: Oxford University Press, 2007.

Duncan, Russell. "Rufus Bullock (1834–1907)." New Georgia Encyclopedia. Accessed November 29, 2015. http://www.georgiaencyclopedia.org/articles/government-politics/rufus-bullock-1834-1907.

Fisher, Isaac. "The Funeral of Booker T. Washington." Booker T. Washington Society. Accessed December 9, 2015. http://www.btwsociety.org/library/honors/05.php.

Gibson, Robert A. "Booker T. Washington and W. E. B. DuBois: The Problem of Negro Leadership." Yale-New Haven Teachers Institute. Accessed November 18, 2015. http://www.yale.edu/ynhti/curriculum/units/1978/2/78.02.02.x.html.

Google Answers. "The Price of Cotton 1800-2000: A Table." Accessed November 17, 2015. http://answers.google.com/answers/threadview/id/33770.html.

Hampton University. "Hampton University: History." Accessed November 11, 2015. http://www.hamptonu.edu/about/history.cfm.

History Matters. "Booker T. Washington Delivers the 1895 Atlanta Compromise Speech." Accessed November 11, 2015. http://www.historymatters.gmu.edu/d/39.

———. "W. E. B. Dubois Critiques Booker T. Washington." Accessed November 11, 2015. http://historymatters.gmu.edu/d/40.

Jackson, David H., Jr. *Booker T. Washington and the Struggle against White Supremacy: The Southern Educational Tours, 1908–1912.* New York: Palgrave Macmillan, 2008.

Jean-Laurent, Annabella. "At the Cusp between Post-Civil War Reconstruction and the Early Struggle for Civil Rights." Negro Building Remembrance Competition. Accessed December 5, 2015. http://www.negrobuildingcompetition.com/the-negro-building.

National Park Service. "Booker T. Washington National Monument." Accessed November 11, 2015. http://www.nps.gov/bowa/index.htm.

Norrell, Robert J. *Up from History: The Life of Booker T. Washington*. Cambridge, MA: The Belknap Press of Harvard University Press, 2009.

Sanneh, Kelefa. "The Wizard." *New Yorker*, February 2, 2009. Accessed November 1, 2015. http://www.newyorker.com/magazine/2009/02/02/the-wizard.

Schroeder, Alan. *Booker T. Washington: Educator and Racial Spokesman*. Black Americans of Achievement. New York: Chelsea House, 1992.

Smock, Raymond W., ed. *Booker T. Washington in Perspective: Essays of Louis R. Harlan*. Jackson, MS: University Press of Mississippi, 1988.

Smock, Raymond W. *Booker T. Washington: Black Leadership in the Age of Jim Crow*. Chicago: Ivan R. Dee, 2009.

Stanford University. "Montgomery Bus Boycott (1955-1956.)" King Encyclopedia. Accessed December 11, 2015. http://kingencyclopedia.stanford.edu/encyclopedia/encyclopedia/enc_montgomery_bus_boycott_1955_1956.

Tuskegee University. "History of Tuskegee University." Accessed November 1, 2015. http://www.tuskegee.edu/about_us/history_and_mission.asp.

Ward, David. "100 Years Since Booker T. Washington's Historic Visit to the Mormons." *Deseret News*, March 29, 2013. Accessed November 29, 2015. http://www.deseretnews.com/article/865576864/100-years-since-Booker-T-Washington7s-historic-visit-to-the-Mormons.html?pg=all.

Washington, Booker T. "The Awakening of the Negro." *The Atlantic*, September 1896. Accessed Nov. 1, 2015. http://www.theatlantic.com/past/unbound/flashbks/blacked/washaw.htm.

———. *Up from Slavery*. Mineola, NY: Dover Publications, 1995. First published 1901 by Doubleday, Page and Company.

Index

Page numbers in **boldface** are illustrations. Entries in **boldface** are glossary terms.

About the Author

BUDD BAILEY has been a sports reporter and editor at the *Buffalo News* since 1993. Before that, he worked for the Buffalo Sabres hockey team and WEBR Radio. Budd and his wife, Jody, live in Buffalo, New York. His loves include his family, friends, visiting new places, reading and writing interesting stories, listening to a great new piece of music that he can't wait to hear again, and watching a bases-clearing triple in a baseball game.